MINDSET OF A WINNER

The Character Traits Necessary for a Life of Success – a Life of Excellence

By

Sherry M. Carroll

TABLE OF CONTENTS

Introduction

Do you want to be a winner – a success in life? Almost everyone would answer "Yes" to this question. However, the definition of a winner or a success might be very different for each person. Some people will only define success as amassing a large financial sum. Others relate success to being the most knowledgeable in their field. Still others say success is having a lot of true friends.

Whatever your definition of success, there are some character traits which are essential. In this book, I have included thirteen (13) traits which I believe to be crucial. The thirteen traits form the acrostic: "CHARACTER WINS." These character traits are important for anyone regardless of their end goal – whether they are a business person, a student, an employer, a blue-collar worker, or a stay-at-home mom. These traits will help everyone develop the mindset of a winner.

You can go on the internet to search for "character traits of winners" and find lists ranging from four traits to forty traits. Some will cite scientific research supporting their findings, and others base it on their own personal observations. There is an overlap of the traits on different lists.

I have chosen thirteen traits which I consider necessary to be a real success – however you define it. As a Christian, I believe that one of the most important things in life is how we relate to others – "love one another" and "love your neighbor as yourself." Therefore, the majority of the traits in this book involve communication and interaction with others.

To highlight each trait, there are quotes which you can easily write down and use every day. This will help to remind you of the importance of the trait. Each character trait also includes a brief overview of at least one modern (or recent history) person who exhibited that trait, as well as one Bible person who exhibited the trait. Most importantly, each chapter has some ideas, tips, or exercises to help you cultivate that trait in yourself.

I believe that anyone can learn to develop the mindset of a winner, and the aim of this book is to highlight 13 traits that will allow you to do exactly this. You can easily read through the whole book in one sitting. However, it is important to take the time to consider and work on each trait, one at a time, and then move on to the next.

The traits are not in the order of importance; they are in the order of the acrostic! So, you may choose to work on the traits in any order.

I personally believe that the last trait, Spirituality, can help you cultivate all the other traits. It is your personal decision if you want to begin with that one.

Thank you for reading this book; I hope you gain many insights that will help you improve your own character traits so that you too will be seen as a winner and will be prepared for excellence!

Sherry M. Carroll

The Mindset of a Winner

People who display the mindset of a winner, often display many similar character traits. If you do any type of research on this topic, you will discover that there are multiple lists of winning traits. This book includes thirteen of the most important ones that you should concentrate on developing first.

The American Heritage Dictionary (ahdictionary.com) defines trait as: *a distinguishing feature, as of a person's character.*

Vocabulary.com says *"a trait is something about you that makes you 'you.' ... a trait is an important part of someone's personality or appearance. Try to describe your favorite teacher in three words and you'll probably come up with a list of her essential traits – such as compassionate, calm, and kooky."*

Everyone has their own personality, and life would be boring if we were all the same. What you need to learn is how to take your own personality and then nurture it with the character traits outlined in this book.

It is normal to be concerned about how we look on the outside, and it is okay to think about that. It becomes a problem if that is our only concern. How we are on the inside – our character – must be a major part of our development. John C. Maxwell writes on character on his website www.johnmaxwellonleadership.com:

I have often observed people who seemed to be doing all the right things on the outside, yet they were not experiencing success. When that happens, I usually conclude that something is wrong on the inside and needs to be changed. The right motions outwardly with wrong motives inwardly will not bring lasting progress. Right outward talking with wrong inward thinking will not bring lasting success. Expressions of care on the outside with a heart of hatred or contempt on the inside will not bring lasting peace. Continual growth and lasting success are the result of aligning the inside and the outside of our lives. And getting the inside right must come first—with solid character traits that provide the foundation for growth.

When you work to cultivate the 13 character traits included in this book and develop the mindset of a winner, you will have the tools necessary to be a successful person and be prepared for excellence.

> "Be more concerned with your character than your reputation, because your character is what you really are, while your reputation is merely what others think you are." – John Wooden

C – Compassionate

Definitions:

- Compassion - Deep awareness of the suffering of another coupled with the wish to relieve it

- Compassionate – Feeling or showing compassion

Being Compassionate Is Essential for Winners

For most of us, it is easy to show concern when someone is sick or for people caught in a bad situation. However, truly compassionate people go further. Empathy and concern have the awareness and care for the person, but compassion wants to help. The compassionate person will go beyond the recognition and feeling, and they will offer to relieve or rectify the troubling situations (if it is in their power).

Life is hard! One minute everything is fine, but then a car runs a red light and slams into our car or we suddenly get sick or our pet dies. Things happen to all of us every day. We soon discover that we need each other to make it through the difficulties.

The importance of compassion is found in almost every religious tradition – it is usually considered one of the greatest virtues.

There have been scientific studies that suggest actual physiological benefits to practicing compassion:

- Pleasure circuits in the brain are activated when people practice compassion, which leads to more personal happiness.

- People who are generally more compassionate seem to produce more of the hormone DHEA. This hormone counteracts the aging process as well as a percentage of the "stress hormone" (cortisol).

- Compassion boosts the positive effects of the vagus nerve which can slow our heart rate and reduce the risk of heart disease.

- Compassionate people tend to be more optimistic and supportive when communicating with others.

> *"TOO OFTEN WE UNDERESTIMATE THE POWER OF A TOUCH, A SMILE, A KIND WORD, A LISTENING EAR, AN HONEST COMPLIMENT, OR THE SMALLEST ACT OF CARING, ALL OF WHICH HAVE THE POTENTIAL TO TURN A LIFE AROUND."*
>
> **— LEO BUSCAGLIA**

When it comes to the business world, it has been shown time and time again that employers who show compassion to their employees are more likely to have a well-run operation. Research has shown that taking the time to improve working conditions and boost morale will increase productivity substantially.

This can be seen in a company that offers a daycare facility on their premises. Employees have an easy place to drop off their children each day without having to run to the other end of town.

Other examples of compassion in the workplace are shown when employers set up a health facility or even a small gym. Employees can improve their health by using the gym before or after work. A nurse in the workplace allows people to go for blood work or receive weekly allergy shots without taking major time off work.

Quotes about Compassion

"Until he extends the circle of his compassion to all living things, man will not himself find peace." – Albert Schweitzer

"There is no exercise better for the heart than reaching down and lifting people up." – John Holmes

"Compassion is the basis of morality." – Arthur Schopenhauer

"If you want others to be happy, practice compassion. If you want to be happy, practice compassion." – Dalai Lama

"Finally, all of you, be like-minded, be sympathetic, love one another, be compassionate and humble." – I Peter 3:9 (New International Version Bible)

Example of a Person Who Exhibits Compassion – Modern

Mother Teresa is a great example of someone who showed compassion. She is recognized as a modern day saint because she identified and offered compassion to people who were unloved and destitute. She lived from 1910 to 1997 and voluntarily lived a life in poverty so she could be of service to the poor.

Mother Teresa's mother always opened her home to the destitute people in their town. The poor were invited to come to dinner at their home.

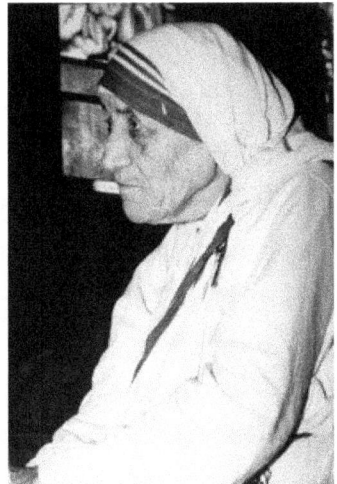

She taught her daughter well and told her: "My child, never eat a single mouthful unless you are sharing it with others." After questioning her mother about who these people were, she was told, "Some of them are our relations, but all of them are our people."

Mother Teresa founded the Missionaries of Charity which runs hospices, homes for people with HIV/AIDS, leprosy and tuberculosis; soup kitchens; mobile clinics; orphanages; and schools. Members of the order must vow to give "wholehearted free service to the poorest of the poor."

Example of a Person Who Exhibits Compassion – Bible

A man was going down from Jerusalem to Jericho, when he was attacked by robbers. They stripped him of his clothes, beat him and went away, leaving him half dead. A priest happened to be going down the same road, and when he saw the man, he passed by on the other side. So too, a Levite, when he came to the place and saw him, passed by on the other side. But a Samaritan, as he traveled, came where the man was; and when he saw him, he took pity on him. He went to him and bandaged his wounds, pouring on oil and wine. Then he put the man on his own donkey, brought him to an inn and took care of him. The next day he took out two denarii and gave them to the innkeeper. 'Look after him,' he said, 'and when I return, I will reimburse you for any extra expense you may have.' – Luke 10:30-35 (New International Version Bible)

The Samaritan saw a man who had been beaten and robbed and left on the side of the road. The Samaritan had compassion on the man, took care of his wounds, and took him to an inn – even paying for the man's boarding and promising to pay more if needed.

Cultivating Compassion

It is possible to become more compassionate. A study at the Center for Investigating Healthy Minds from the University of Wisconsin-Madison found that compassion "can be enhanced with training and practice."

Compassion has 3 parts:

1. recognizing the pain of others,

2. feeling concern/sympathy for others, and

3. seeking to alleviate the pain – even if it is only a small amount – whenever possible.

The first step is to recognize the pain or emotions of others. When we are able to really recognize the pain of others, it is easier to be compassionate. The following exercise, although quite simple, might not be easy. It could induce some emotion; increasing your capacity for empathy and concern is worth it though.

Imagine something terrible happening to a loved one – nothing fatal, but a big problem they must deal with. Write it down (e.g., your cousin goes bankrupt). Next, write down, in as great detail as you can, the pain and suffering they are going through. Repeating this exercise with a variety of scenarios will make feeling empathy second nature to you. It is a first step towards compassion.

> *"Our human compassion binds us the one to the other – not in pity or patronizingly, but as human beings who have learnt how to turn our common suffering into hope for the future."*
> **– Nelson Mandela**

Another exercise to develop compassion is looking for similarities. You can easily recognize the differences between yourself and others, but you can actually help build compassion by making an effort to recognize the commonalities.

In this exercise, you are challenged to find similarities with people you dislike. On the left hand side of a piece of paper, list people you don't like; it could be someone in your daily life or celebrities or politicians, etc. On the right hand side, write what you may have in common.

An example for this exercise: Maybe you dislike Justin Bieber, so you write his name down on the left side. On the right side, you might write things such as: we both have great hair, we both like Selena Gomez, we both love music. Repeat this for several people you dislike.

With this simple exercise, you will begin to program your mind to recognize similarities instead of being so quick to recognize differences. Compassion will come more naturally as you can recognize that all humans have something in common with you.

The last exercise involves practicing generosity. Find a need that you can meet. It might be volunteering at a local charity, doing an errand or a chore for a friend who is overwhelmed, or just lending a listening ear to someone who needs to talk about their problem. Do something kind that will help ease the suffering of someone else. As this becomes a little easier, try to add this into your daily life. Every day, find some way to practice compassion. With repetition, this will become a more automatic response to the problems and pain you see around you.

H – Helpful

Definition:

- Helpful – providing assistance; giving or rendering aid or assistance; making it easier to do a job, deal with a problem, etc.; giving help

Being Helpful Is Essential for Winners

Being helpful means that you are choosing to make a difference by doing something that will be of use to someone else. Some examples would be providing a service, making life easier in some way, doing something for others which they cannot do for themselves, or doing something for others who don't have time to do it for themselves.

When we help each other, we get more done. We make our lives easier. Many people are helpful in some way or another. While this is a trait that a lot of people have, this chapter will help you see how helpfulness can be good for your business or service.

For most businesses, the owner and employees recognize the importance of being helpful to the customers and providing great customer service. With this, the goal is to increase the business and the income. But, it is good to think of other ways to be helpful, without always getting payment for your time?

The January 2014 snowstorm in the southern United States provides an example of a business that was helpful without asking for anything in return. As the interstates and highways became parking lots in the storm in Birmingham, Alabama, a Chick-fil-A restaurant began helping. Employees had been sent home, but many returned because they couldn't go anywhere.

The staff of the Chick-fil-A cooked several hundred sandwiches and walked along the highway handing out sandwiches to everyone they could get to. And, they refused to take any money for the sandwiches.

In addition, Chick-fil-A opened its dining room for anyone who wanted to come in and sleep on a bench or booth. In the morning, the staff cooked several hundred more chicken biscuits to hand out – for free – to the stranded motorists.

Organizations and businesses have found that providing relevant helpfulness will attract customers, and it will also keep them loyal.

Although this example is focused on businesses, it is true for everyone. Try to find ways that you can be viewed as being helpful. In addition to helping others, it can also help you build relationships.

Quotes about Helpfulness

"Do all the good that you can, in all the places you can, in all the ways that you can, at all the times you can, to all the people you can, for as long as you can." – John Wesley

"I don't know what your destiny will be, but one thing I do know: the only ones among you who will be really happy are those who have sought and found how to serve." – Albert Schweitzer

"I think I began learning long ago that those who are happiest are those who do the most for others." – Booker T. Washington

"We can't help everyone, but everyone can help someone." – Dr. Loretta Scott

"Successful people are always looking for opportunities to help others. Unsuccessful people are always asking, 'What's in it for me?'" – Brian Tracy

"What good is it, my brothers and sisters, if someone claims to have faith but has no deeds? Can such faith save them? Suppose a brother or a sister is without clothes and daily food. If one of you says to them, 'Go in peace; keep warm and well fed,' but does nothing about their physical needs, what good is it? In the same way, faith by itself, if it is not accompanied by action, is dead." – James 2:14-17 (New International Version Bible)

Example of a Person Who Exhibits Helpfulness – Modern

Clarissa "Clara" Barton is a well-known woman from American history. She was working as a clerk in the U.S. Patent Office in Washington, D.C. when the Civil War began.

Barton recognized a need among the men in the military – seeing many were wounded and/or hungry, some had no bedding, and some had no clothes other than what they were wearing. Barton began taking supplies to young men who were temporarily housed in the unfinished Capitol building. She provided clothing, food, and supplies to sick and wounded soldiers.

Barton collected some supplies on her own, appealed to the public for help, and created a system to store and distribute the supplies. In addition to supplies, Barton provided personal support to the young men by reading to them, writing letters for them, listening when they needed to talk, and praying with them.

Barton recognized that help was most needed on the battlefield. So, instead of remaining with the medical units which were kept far back from the fights, she went right into the battle. She would go around on the battlefield nursing and comforting the wounded.

Even after the war, Barton continued to find ways to help. She established the Office of Correspondence with Friends of the Missing Men of the United States Army in her own home and helped identify over 22,000 missing men.

Later, through her leadership and influence with three different U.S. Presidents, the American Red Cross was established, receiving its first congressional charter in 1900.

Example of a Person Who Exhibits Helpfulness – Bible

"In Joppa there was a disciple named Tabitha (in Greek her name is Dorcas); she was always doing good and helping the poor. ...

"Peter went with them, and when he arrived he was taken upstairs to the room. All the widows stood around him, crying and showing him the robes and other clothing that Dorcas had made while she was still with them." – Acts 9:36, 39 (New International Version Bible)

Tabitha (Greek name: Dorcas) was always being helpful and doing good. In addition to helping the poor, she had made robes and clothing for many widows.

Cultivating Helpfulness

It is very easy to find ways to be helpful. Helping does not need to be a huge expensive project. Here are some very simple ways to help:

- Offer to help with a task a neighbor is doing (e.g., trimming hedges, raking leaves)

- Take a friend (or colleague) to lunch and pick up the tab

- Listen, without interrupting, when someone wants to share a story or problem

- Provide a resource which will be useful, such as an interesting article, to a co-worker

The best way to cultivate helpfulness is to be helpful! Make plans to do this daily. Here are 3 steps:

1. Help someone close to you today – even if it is just taking a cup of coffee to a co-worker to boost their spirits. Make notes afterwards: Who did you help and how did you help them?

2. Offer help to someone you know who needs it. We all know someone who needs help. Take the first step and offer to help them. Make notes: Who really needs my help and how can I help them?

3. Now, step up to some serious helping. Do some research in your local community or online to find an important cause to support. It should be something or someone that really touches you. Research who you want to help (organization, person or cause) and choose one to help any way you can! Again, make notes: What is the cause or person to support and how will I help them?

The important thing is to seek to be helpful to someone <u>on a daily basis</u> – including family, not just outsiders.

Now all that is left is to actually go help some people! Bonus - this is a great way to keep your positive attitude boosted, which is another character trait to be covered in a later chapter!

> *"I'm touched by the idea that when we do things that are useful and helpful – collecting these shards of spirituality – that we may be helping to bring about a healing"* - **Leonard Nimoy**

A –Ambition

Definitions:

- Ambition: *(noun)* an earnest desire for some type of achievement or distinction, as wealth or fame, and the willingness to strive for it; strong desire for success, achievement, or distinction

- Ambitious: *(adjective)* having ambition; eagerly desirous of achieving or obtaining success, power, wealth, etc.; strongly desirous

Having Ambition Is Essential for Winners

Most people have some form of ambition in their lives. Even young children demonstrate ambition by wanting to become a superhero, soldier, president or doctor when they get older.

Leading a happier life can come from fulfilling your ambitions. Meeting your goals and expectations has actually been shown to help people live longer too!

You may have an ambition to get a better paying job or start your own business. You still need to take action to make this a reality. Ambitious people do not wait for things to come to them; instead they go out and get them. Learn how to set goals and how to acquire the skills necessary to reach them.

It is also important to recognize that ambition does not mean going after your goals to the detriment of yourself and others. Becoming a tyrant who climbs over others, or filling your life with stress and burn-out due to 16-hour work days is not going to make you a person of excellence or give you true success.

Ambitious does not equal ruthless! Although people often equate ambition with a drive for honor, fame, money, or power, true ambition is the drive to improve, develop, and create.

True ambition involves three things: goals or dreams, drive, and skills.

Quotes about Ambition

"Intelligence without ambition is a bird without wings." – Salvador Dali

"Ambition is the germ from which all growth of nobleness proceeds." – Oscar Wilde

"Ambition has one heel nailed in well, though she stretch her fingers to touch the heavens." – Lao Tzu

"Boys, be ambitious. Be ambitious not for money, not for selfish aggrandizement, not for the evanescent thing which men call fame. Be ambitious for the attainment of all that a man can be." – William Clark

"Brothers and sisters, I do not consider myself yet to have taken hold of it. But one thing I do: Forgetting what is behind and straining toward what is ahead, I press on toward the goal to win the prize for which God has called me heavenward in Christ Jesus." – Philippians 3:13-14 (New International Version Bible)

Example of a Person Who Exhibits Ambition – Modern

Helen Keller is a person who showed a tremendous amount of ambition in her life. By the age of two she was deaf and blind and still went on to become the first deaf blind person to earn a Bachelor of Arts degree.

Helen Keller became a prolific author, writing 12 books and numerous articles. She was a political activist and campaigned for women's suffrage, pacifism, labor rights and other causes during her lifetime. She helped found the American Civil Liberties Union in 1920.

Keller spent 25 years learning to speak so that others could understand her. She traveled to over 30 countries as a world-famous speaker, taking inspiration and encouragement to millions.

She lacked the ability to see and hear – but she didn't lack ambition! Helen Keller's ambition allowed her to overcome the unbelievable obstacles she faced.

Example of a Person Who Exhibits Ambition – Bible

King Solomon was a very ambitious person in the Bible. He reigned over Jerusalem for forty years and had many ambitious building projects during his years.

- In the fourth year of his reign, he began building a Temple of the Lord. The blocks were all prepared at the quarry, and no hammer, chisel, or other iron tool was used at the Temple site. Solomon had the interior walls lined with cedar; and many areas of the interior of the temple, including the floors were overlaid with pure gold. It took seven years to complete the building. (I Kings 6)

- Solomon built a Palace, which took thirteen years. There was a throne room, a Hall of Justice where he judged, and a living area. In addition, there was a palace or separate living area for the Pharaoh's daughter, whom he married. (I Kings 7)

- Solomon built several cities including Hazor, Megiddo, Gezer, Lower Beth Horon, Baalath, and Tadmor, along with store cities and towns for his chariots and his horses. (I Kings 9:15-19)

- Solomon also built ships. (I Kings 9:26)

- Solomon accumulated chariots and horses; fourteen hundred chariots and twelve thousand horses. (I Kings 10:26)

"King Solomon was greater in riches and wisdom than all the other kings of the earth." – I Kings 10:23 (New International Version Bible)

Looking at this, it appears that Solomon's ambition was simply to acquire wealth and property. However, when Solomon was given the chance to ask for anything from God, Solomon's request was for a discerning heart to rule the people and to distinguish right from wrong. I Kings 4:29-30 says, *"God gave Solomon wisdom and very great insight, and a breadth of understanding as measureless as the sand on the seashore. Solomon's wisdom was greater than the wisdom of all the people of the East, and greater than all the wisdom of Egypt."*

Cultivating Ambition

As mentioned above, ambition involves three things; and the first one is goals or dreams. Many times, a lack of ambition comes down to the fact that people don't really know what they want to do. It is hard to have ambition and drive if you don't have a destination or focus.

The first step, if you want to cultivate ambition, is to determine what your ideal life is: what is your dream or goal for your life? Don't worry about the details for a moment. Step back and begin cultivating ambition by defining your ultimate life. Take some time (not just a few minutes; take some real time) and envision your ideal life. If you had the successful or excellent life you want, what would your life be like?

Grab a pad and paper and start writing. There is no wrong or right answer for this exercise. The key is to be as specific and vivid as you can be. Do this now!

Once you have mapped out your ideal life, you will naturally feel more driven to accomplish it. Seriously! Stop and think about how you feel right now after writing that? Don't you feel at least a slight tingling to go get that life right now? That's ambition! Read your vision for an ideal life daily; think about it and try to visualize it as often as possible. Revise it if needed. When you do this, you will feed the fires that fuel your ambition.

The third part of ambition is skills. Now that you have a vision of your successful life and you have begun to feel the drive, it is time to start developing the skills. Each person has a different dream, so the skills you may need will be different than the ones another person will need. But, get started learning the necessary skills. You may take online courses, go back to college, work with a trainer, or something else. Whatever is needed, begin learning the skills you need to fuel your ambition.

"Big results require big ambition."
— **Heraclitus**

R – Respect for Self and Others

Definitions

- Respect: to feel or show deferential regard for; esteem; willingness to show consideration or appreciation; to treat courteously or kindly

- Respectfulness: showing or marked by proper respect; characterized by or showing politeness or deference

Having Respect for Self and Others Is Essential for Winners

If you ask people how they wish to be treated by others, one item which is usually near the top of everyone's list is to be treated with dignity and respect. Professor Jonathan Haidt, a professor at New York University Stern School of Business, says that respect for tradition and legitimate authority is one of five fundamental moral values shared by most societies and individuals.

Respect is shown by considering the person's feelings before reacting, treating the other person with kindness and courtesy, truly listening when another person speaks, showing patience and humility with others, and using good manners. Showing respect also means allowing others to deal with (or solve) problems without telling them what they MUST do and without underestimating them.

Respect can be given and received by individuals. We often think of respect as something that is earned. However, an individual can show respect to another even if the other person has done nothing worthy of respect.

As the Josephson Institute (www.josephsoninstitute.org) points out:

"It is not that every person deserves to be treated with respect. In fact, I think that people who blatantly disregard the dignity and humanity of others forfeit whatever 'right' to respect they may have had. Mass murderers, mothers who kill their children, gangsters who kill or maim innocent people in mindless drive-by shootings ... to name a few, relinquish any possible claim that they are entitled to be treated with respect. Yet I believe that each of us has an inviolable moral duty to treat them and others with respect. This duty is not based on their rights but on our responsibility to be better than they are.

"I am reminded of a story about two politicians in bitter debate. When one became abusive and insulting, the other replied, 'Sir, I will continue to treat you like a gentleman. Not because you are, but because I am one.' It is our humanity, not theirs, we affirm when we treat all people with respect."

Showing respect does not mean we agree with or endorse what another person does or what they believe. You can disagree with their words or actions without becoming disagreeable yourself.

When someone shows respect, they will more easily gain cooperation from others. If there is respect between people, there are fewer conflicts. When there is respect, people listen to each other's opinions, so there is the opportunity to learn from each other – whether it is learning information or skills or learning a different perspective for viewing a situation or problem. And, when a person shows respect to others, they will usually receive respect in return.

It is easy to say what happens when there is lack of respect between people. When there is no respect, there is often dishonesty, feeling misunderstood, bullying, contempt, and feeling like you are not heard.

> "Respect for ourselves guides our morals, respect for others guides our manners."
> – Laurence Sterne

Respect for others does not mean that you give up all your own rights. In fact, many psychologists believe that you cannot respect others if you do not respect yourself. People with self-respect will assert themselves and will not allow themselves or others to be treated badly. People with self-respect will take care of their own physical and emotional needs without being so focused on pleasing others and getting their approval.

There is a difference between fear and respect. Some people might show deference to another or obey them because of fear rather than respect. But, fear is harmful while respect is nurturing. Fear will destroy self-confidence while respect will build it. Fear is forced while respect is freely given.

Quotes about Respect/Respectfulness

"Let every man be respected as an individual and no man idolized." – Albert Einstein

"I am not concerned with your liking or disliking me ...All I ask is that you respect me as a human being." – Jackie Robinson

"One of the most sincere forms of respect is actually listening to what another has to say." – Bryant H. McGill

"I firmly believe that respect is a lot more important, and a lot greater, than popularity." – Julius Erving

"Without feelings of respect, what is there to distinguish men from beasts?" – Confucius

"The final test of a gentleman is his respect for those who can be of no possible service to him." – William Lyon Phelps

"Show proper respect to everyone, love the family of believers, fear God, honor the emperor." – I Peter 2:17 (New International Version Bible)

Example of a Person Who Exhibits Respect for Self and Others – Modern

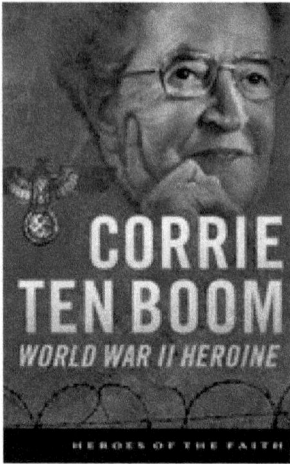

Cornelia "Corrie" Ten Boom was a Dutch watchmaker – the first licensed female watchmaker in her country. Ten Boom lived with her parents and sister in Haarlem, Netherlands.

Corrie Ten Boom demonstrated respect for all people. She ran a church for mentally disabled people and raised foster children in her home. Everyone was special to her.

In 1940, the Nazis invaded the Netherlands. As the Nazis began arresting and killing Jews, the Ten Booms began a "hiding place," opening their home to refugees (Jews and members of the resistance). Corrie became the leader in the underground network in Haarlem.

Until their arrest in February 1944, Corrie and her family were able to save at least 800 Jews, along with protecting underground workers. When the Ten Booms were arrested, there were 6 people in the secret room in their house who remained safe and escaped later.

Example of a Person Who Exhibits Respect for Self and Others – Bible

Two Israelite men went into the town of Jericho to check it out. The men of the town tried to find the Israelites in order to kill them. Rahab hid the two men so they would not be killed. Even though the men were foreigners, she showed respect for them by protecting them and helping them escape.

The story is in Joshua 2. In chapter 6, Rahab is rewarded for her help by saving her and all of her family when Jericho is captured.

Cultivating Respect for Self and Others

Respect can be shown through our actions. At the same time, we may feel respect for others. This book cannot change your feelings, but there are some practical actions you can take to show respect through your behavior.

There are many actions which demonstrate respect for others, and you could choose any of these as the focus for cultivating respect. Here is a list of several actions you can work on:

- Use common courtesy words, such as "please" and "thank you." Being polite doesn't cost you anything, but it can help brighten the mood of others as you acknowledge them.

- Address someone by their name. When you take the time to learn someone's name, even someone you only see occasionally (such as the mail carrier, the janitor in your office building, etc.) and you use their name, you are showing them respect and personally acknowledging them.

- Watch your language. Think about some disrespectful words or phrases or profanity that you tend to use. Do you resort to finger-pointing or rude words when you get more stressed? Use neutral, descriptive words in place of the negative words.

- Use more compliments or encouragement. Praise more frequently than you criticize. Try to find at least one person each day to give a compliment to.

- Actively listen when others are talking. Instead of planning what you will say or thinking of all the other things you need to do, give the other person your full attention. Be attentive and give good feedback – the other person will see that you are truly listening and showing them respect.

- Recognize that people are emotional creatures. Even if the feelings don't seem to make sense to you (you don't know why they feel that way), seek to understand their feelings, know that their feelings matter, and take their feelings into consideration.

- Solicit and allow feedback. Encourage others to express their opinions and ideas. Do not exclude someone because you assume they will not have any helpful suggestions.

- Show an interest in things that are important to others. Ask them about their family or their pets or their hobbies. Getting to know some small detail about the person takes a little initiative, but it shows respect for the person.

- If you are a leader, model civility and respect for others. Clearly define the expectations for respectful behavior.

"As all human beings are, in my view, creatures of God's design, we must respect all other human beings. That does not mean I have to agree with their choices or agree with their opinions, but indeed I respect them as human beings." – Stockwell Day

A – Authentic/Sincere

Definitions:

- Authentic: accurate in representation of the facts; worthy of trust, reliance, or belief

- Authenticity: the quality of being authentic, trustworthy, or genuine

- Sincere: not feigned or affected; genuine

- Sincerity: the quality or state of being free from pretense, deceit or hypocrisy; honesty in expression; genuineness, honesty, and freedom from duplicity

Being Authentic or Sincere Is Essential for Winners

It is important to be honest and genuine – without deceit or hypocrisy – no matter what you do in life. You must be honest with yourself and with others and take responsibility for your own mistakes. This is true for both your business dealings as well as in your personal life.

Being authentic of sincere includes being honest or true to yourself; this is particularly important. You have your own set of values and beliefs and you should never weaken these by going against them.

This is not always easy. There are times when being true to your own values and what you believe is right means that you will go against the crowd.

There are benefits to being authentic and sincere:

- You will earn the respect of others because you stand by your own beliefs and values

- Who you are, what you do, and what you believe in are all in alignment

- Being authentic to yourself is less stressful than trying to be someone you are not

When you are being sincere and authentic, you will mean what you say and practice what you preach.

If you are authentic and sincere, you will work to deliver the highest quality service or products that you are able to for your clients or customers. The time you take to put in care, consideration and effort into your work will show. Customers will appreciate the hard work and will be happy to provide recommendations. You will earn the respect and loyalty of your clients, customers and business associates when you stay sincere and authentic.

Part of authenticity is meaning what you say! Don't be a "yes" man. Don't tell people what they want to hear. You are a winner; it is important to act like one! Tell people how you feel, be straightforward and you will be able to stand by your word.

A sincere individual values himself, takes the tasks assigned seriously, and seeks ways to execute his responsibilities with utmost diligence and perfection.

Quotes about Authenticity or Sincerity

"Hold faithfulness and sincerity as first principles." – Confucius

"Sincerity makes the very least person to be of more value than the most talented hypocrite." – Charles Spurgeon

"How would your life be different if ... you approached all relationships with authenticity and honesty? Let today be the day ... you dedicate yourself to building relationships on the solid foundation of truth and authenticity." – Steve Maraboli

"Nothing is more attractive than being your authentic self!" – Dawn Gluskin

"Truly being authentic is knowing what matters to you, on the deepest level of who you are, and committing always to act from that authentic center." – Richie Norton

"Sincerity is not only effective and honourable, it is also much less difficult than is commonly supposed." – George Henry Lewes

"The privilege of a lifetime is to become who you truly are." – C.G. Jung

"The goal of this command is love, which comes from a pure heart and a good conscience and a sincere faith." – I Timothy 1:5 (New International Version Bible)

Example of a Person Who Exhibits Authenticity or Sincerity – Modern

Betty Ford is someone who demonstrated authenticity in her life. Once she became the First Lady, she was thrust into a leadership position. She was known for her openness and candor. She did not change her core values in her new position as First Lady.

Betty Ford was open and sincere when she was diagnosed with breast cancer, and used the opportunity to show the public that it is okay to have a disease that needs treatment. She could have kept quiet about her struggles, but chose to be authentic – to help provide comfort for other women fighting the disease.

In later years, when Betty Ford struggled with alcoholism and addiction to prescription drugs, she spoke publicly of her struggles. Her authenticity encouraged others to deal with their issues as well.

Example of a Person Who Exhibits Authenticity or Sincerity – Bible

Samuel exhibited authenticity even as a young man. As a young boy, Samuel was sent to serve with the priest Eli. Eli had two sons who were also priests. Eli's sons were wicked and did many bad things. But, Samuel did not change his actions or attitudes even as he was faced with the wickedness of these two priests.

"And the boy Samuel continued to grow in stature and in favor with the Lord and with people." – I Samuel 2:26 (New International Version Bible)

In later years, when Saul has become the first King of Israel, Samuel is the priest. Saul is a mighty warrior. Instead of waiting for Samuel in I Samuel 13, Saul decides to carry out duties set aside for the priests alone. When Samuel finds out, he speaks up immediately rebuking the king. Samuel continues to be true to his beliefs and values, even when facing the King.

> *"Today you are you, that is truer than true. There is no one alive who is Youer than You."*
> **– Dr. Seuss**

Cultivating Authenticity or Sincerity

In order to be authentic and sincere, you have to be yourself, no matter who you are with. Are you the same when you are alone, when you are at work, when you are with acquaintances, and when you are with close friends? If you are trying to act the way you think other people want you to act, you are not being sincere. And, you are working too hard!

In other chapters – especially the chapter on integrity – we talk about knowing your own values and beliefs. This is part of sincerity. You have to know who you are in order to act in that way all the time. Whatever you do or say, it should come from your heart.

Sincerity is especially important when you are making an apology. If someone perceives your apology to be insincere, they will reject it.

We all make mistakes and that leads to a time when we need to apologize. This exercise is going to help you craft a sincere apology. To make a sincere apology, you must acknowledge that what you did was wrong, accept responsibility for your action, make attempts to atone (if possible) for the wrong, and give assurances that you won't do it again.

Here are four questions you can answer to help you craft a sincere apology (with an example for each). Putting it in writing first will help you when you are ready to deliver the apology.

1. Who do you need to apologize to?
   [example: my wife]

2. What did you do that was wrong?
   [example: I told her she looked fat]

3. Why were you responsible for that?
   [example: It was a thoughtless thing to say. I should never make her feel ugly because she is beautiful to me!]

4. Why won't it happen again?
   [example: I realize it hurt her. I will be much more careful of

the words I use because I don't have the right to make her feel bad. I love her and will dedicate my focus to making sure I never make her feel horrible again.]

Number 3 is very important if you are seeking to make a sincere apology. People want to see you admit your mistake and take responsibility for your actions. This is the point when most people will recognize this as a sincere apology.

Once you have filled out those four questions, you have an apology ready to use. You know who you need to apologize too, what you did wrong and why it will never happen again. All that is left is to deliver it to them.

Here are some tips as you head out to apologize:

- Give people some space/time before apologizing. Sometimes people need to calm down and get control of their emotions before they will be receptive to even the most sincere of apologies. (This doesn't mean to wait 2 weeks to apologize, but a day or two may be needed.)

- When you acknowledge the wrong you did, let the person know that you understand all the difference consequences of your actions (personal, emotional, monetary, etc.)

- Be specific - tell them exactly what you are apologizing for. Do not add feelings you think you might have caused in the other person (I'm sorry your feelings were hurt) because this shifts the blame/focus from you taking responsibility for your own actions.

- Don't expect anything in return. If you only apologize to gain forgiveness or attention, you are being insincere!

- Mean what you say, and commit to being better.

C – Courageous

Definitions:

- Courage: the state or quality of mind or spirit that enables one to face danger, fear, or challenges with self-possession, confidence, and resolution; bravery; being resolute in the face of challenges

- Courageous: having or characterized by courage

Being Courageous Is Essential for Winners

Many times we think of courage in relation to physical bravery, such as the soldier who continues on as the bullets fly around him. But, courage is not just physical bravery. Standing up against injustice, taking financial risks to follow your dream, sticking to your own values when others are disparaging, overcoming difficulties and disabilities to endure and conquer, stepping up to take responsibility for a mistake, challenging existing ideas which are generally accepted but may be wrong ... these are all examples of courage.

A person who demonstrates courage is often viewed as a bold person. This type of person may not show much anxiety or frustration when it comes to dealing with the challenges in everyday life.

While being courageous is one thing, this is a trait which you don't want to overdo. People who go overboard in displaying courage can become reckless or get into dangerous circumstances.

To be successful in life you need to demonstrate a solid amount of courage. You must be confident in your decisions and your ability. You do not want to allow others to dissuade you from your actions.

A courageous person will be strong in their own convictions and will be motivated to follow through and get things done.

Being courageous does NOT mean there is no fear. What makes courageous people different is that they don't let the fear stop them. Instead they use the fear to their advantage by not allowing it to become an obstacle. They work on finding ways to get around the obstacle and keep pushing their way through until they reach their final goal.

Quotes about Courage

"I learned that courage was not the absence of fear, but the triumph over it. The brave man is not he who does not feel afraid, but he who conquers that fear." – Nelson Mandela

"He who is not courageous enough to take risks will accomplish nothing in life." – Muhammad Ali

"It takes courage to grow up and become who you really are." – E.E. Cummings

"Courage and perseverance have a magical talisman, before which difficulties disappear and obstacles vanish into air." – John Quincy Adams

"Be strong and courageous. Do not be afraid or terrified because of them, for the Lord your God goes with you; he will never leave you nor forsake you." – Deuteronomy 31:6 (New International Version Bible)

"Be on your guard; stand firm in the faith; be courageous; be strong." – I Corinthians 16:13 (New International Version Bible)

Example of a Person Who Exhibits Courage – Modern

Presidents and leaders of countries often demonstrate courage. Theodore Roosevelt, who is often viewed as one of the greatest U.S. Presidents, demonstrated the trait of courage in many ways. This can be seen in his ability to be confident of his actions and being courageous by following through on his convictions.

Before he became President, Teddy Roosevelt formed the famous Rough Riders. He gained fame for his courage in battle in Cuba during the Spanish-American War.

Teddy Roosevelt took the view that a President should be "the steward of the people" and should take whatever actions were necessary for the good of his people, without breaking the Constitution.

He was the first U.S. President to speak out on conservation, greatly expanding the national parks and forests. He ended up being awarded the Nobel Peace Prize for mediating the Russo-Japanese War.

He worked tirelessly on his convictions and was never afraid to follow his dreams.

Example of a Person Who Exhibits Courage – Bible

Many times in his life, Joshua exhibited courage. When the children of Israel had fled from Egypt and were wandering in the desert, Joshua was one of the twelve men sent to spy out the land. Ten of the men returned to say that the people were too many and too strong and the Israelites should just give up and return to Egypt.

Joshua and Caleb were the only two to speak differently. Joshua said, *"And do not be afraid of the people of the land, because we will devour them. Their protection is gone, but the Lord is with us. Do not be afraid of them."* (Numbers 14:9)

In later years, after Moses dies, Joshua becomes the leader of the Israelites. He courageously leads them through many battles in order to gain their homeland. He inspires the people to follow him, *"Do not be afraid; do not be discouraged. Be strong and courageous."* (Joshua 10:25)

Cultivating Courage

Fear can be a healthy response to true danger. However, as many of the quotes above pointed out, courage is acting even when fearful. Fear can hold you back from your true potential. Misplaced or irrational fear is especially troubling in any efforts to develop the mindset of a winner.

A key step in cultivating the courage to overcome fear is to focus on your goal. When a firefighter enters a burning building to rescue a trapped person, he is focused on the goal of rescue. This allows him to overcome the natural fear of fire.

Here are some steps to take to begin cultivating courage:

1. Write down your fear

2. Write down a goal you want to achieve that is blocked by the fear

3. Write down what you can do to conquer the fear in order to reach the goal

4. Write down what some potential negative outcomes could be as you face the fear with courage, and what can you do to prepare for these

5. Now, step out of your comfort zone and follow through

Here is an example:

- *My fear: speaking in public*

- *Goal: Get a promotion which requires me to make a presentation at a regional meeting*

- *What can I do: I will write and present a speech to my family. Then I will present it to someone other than my family. If I can't find an audience, I will film it and post it to YouTube*

- *Potential outcomes and how to prepare: I am worried that I will stumble over the words of the speech, so I will practice over and over*

Make sure you focus on your goal. This will help you gain the courage needed for the action in spite of the fear. And, don't forget to celebrate when you take your courageous steps to overcome!

> *"YOU GAIN STRENGTH, COURAGE, AND CONFIDENCE BY EVERY EXPERIENCE IN WHICH YOU REALLY STOP TO LOOK FEAR IN THE FACE. YOU ARE ABLE TO SAY TO YOURSELF, 'I LIVED THROUGH THIS HORROR. I CAN TAKE THE NEXT THING THAT COMES ALONG.'"*
> — ELEANOR ROOSEVELT

T – Tact (Think Before You Speak)

Definitions:

- Tact: a keen sense of what to say or do to avoid giving offense; skill in dealing with difficult situations; discretion; diplomacy

- Tactful: possessing or exhibiting tact

Being Tactful Is Essential for Winners

This trait involves taking time to think through what you are going to say before you say it. This trait is one that your parents probably tried to teach you as a child. How many times did you hear, "Think before you speak."?

Even with our parent's attempts to teach us, we have all been guilty of speaking out before thinking about the consequences of our words. If you don't think about what you are going to say before you say it, you could hurt someone's feelings and possibly lose a friend.

Words are very powerful. There is an old idiom "Sticks and stones may break my bones but words will never harm me." It is totally false! A few hurtful words can affect someone for many years. And a few kind words can have a positive effect for a lifetime.

When it comes to being a winner in life you really need to always think about the results of what you are going to say. Many famous people have spoken without thinking, and this has had devastating effects. It can ruin a reputation and even damage or end a career.

The words you choose define who you are. You can choose to guard what you say and use words which are helpful, words which will benefit the person listening. Your choice of tactful communication will strengthen your reputation and build your credibility, showing integrity, professionalism, and maturity.

Today, in this age of social media, it is important to understand that you cannot hide from your words. If you post something to your Facebook wall or send out a Tweet, it is there for all to see. Once something is on the internet, it spreads and is basically impossible to take back.

Quotes about Tact

"Remember not only to say the right thing in the right place, but far more difficult still, to leave unsaid the wrong thing at the tempting moment." – Benjamin Franklin

"Tact is the art of making a point without making an enemy." – Isaac Newton

"Tact is the ability to formulate your thoughts, carefully choose your words and effectively communicate them without offending anyone. This is the most difficult skill to achieve, the best skill anyone can possess, and the most important skill in our daily lives." – Uzoma Nnadi

"It is tact that is golden, not silence." – Samuel Butler

"Let your conversation be always full of grace, seasoned with salt, so that you may know how to answer everyone." – Colossians 4:6 (New International Version Bible)

"A gentle answer turns away wrath, but a harsh word stirs up anger." – Proverbs 15:1 (New International Version Bible)

Example of a Person Who Exhibits Tact – Modern

Martin Luther King, Jr., a well-known American pastor and civil rights leader, exhibited tact many times in his life.

Through the years that he was involved in and led the civil rights movement, he was arrested, jailed, and fined numerous times. His home was bombed. He faced personal harassment, police brutality, and violence from opponents.

Others within the civil rights movement argued that power should be secured by violence and force. However, Martin Luther King Jr. continued to speak of peace, of nonviolence, of equality, and rights. He did not verbally attack others even as they attacked him.

Martin Luther King, Jr. used his speeches to continually call for equality for all, for civil rights. His "I Have a Dream" speech is said to have "awakened the soul of a nation with one of the most important orations in American history" (according to Lucinda Moore, writing "Dream Assignment" in the *Smithsonian Magazine*).

Example of a Person Who Exhibits Tact – Bible

Gideon was a judge over the Israelites. In Judges 7, Gideon leads a small group of 300 men into battle and defeated a large army of Midianites.

In Judges 8:1, the men of Ephraim tried to start a quarrel with Gideon. They "challenged him vigorously." They were upset because Gideon had not included them when he went into battle.

Gideon responded with great tact instead of joining in an argument. He provided an explanation of what happened, as well as offered praise for what the Ephraimites had accomplished. Gideon was calm, modest, and tactful in his response (Judges 8:2-3). This calmed the men and ended any potential arguments.

Cultivating Tact

Thinking before you speak is not something new for us to work on. As mentioned above, most of us had parents trying to teach us in our childhood.

A few exercises from this book probably cannot make you learn to think before you talk. However, here is an exercise which will help you solidify the importance of this lesson.

Take the time now to remember 5-10 times that you spoke before you thought with negative consequences. Write down what you said. Then, write down the negative impact the incident had. Here is an example:

What I said: I told my wife her pants made her look fat.

Negative impact: She got very angry and our interactions have been unpleasant since then.

This list will not fix your problem overnight. However, by the time you get to the end of it, you are going to be more aware of the negative outcomes that come from speaking without thinking.

Here are some tips on how you can think before you speak in the real world:

- Actively think before you say something. Pause to consider how your words will be understood

- In a heated situation make sure you take the time to think before you speak. Follow the common adage, "Count to 10 before you speak."

- Observe more than you speak. This will help you get "into their head" to have a better idea of how they will take what you are going to say.

- Use "T-H-I-N-K" – Before saying something you feel is important run it through your mind to make sure it is **True, Helpful, Inspiring, Necessary,** and **Kind.**

- Pay attention to people's reactions to your words. Don't talk blindly; make note of how people are reacting to your words.

- Think about your tone; sometimes HOW you say something is more important than what you are saying.

Before you speak ...

THINK!

T – is it true?

H – is it helpful?

I – is it inspiring?

N – is it necessary?

K – is it kind?

E – Energetic/Diligent

Definitions:

- Energy: the capacity for work or vigorous activity; vigor; power; intensity or vitality of action

- Energetic: possessing, exerting, or displaying energy; vigorous; active

- Diligent: marked by persevering, painstaking effort; attentive and persistent in doing something

- Diligence: earnest and persistent application to an undertaking; steady effort

Being Energetic or Diligent Is Essential for Winners

By the end of the sixth century, Pope Gregory I had created a list of the "Seven Deadly Sins." To oppose these, a list of the seven heavenly virtues was defined. One of these virtues is diligence. Diligence is considered the opposite of the "deadly sin" of sloth or laziness.

A 2013 book titled *"Daily Rituals: How Artists Work"* by Mason Currey examines the work habits of over 160 novelists, poets, playwrights, painters, philosophers, scientists, and mathematicians. One trait that the vast majority of these people have in common is diligence ... in fact, the majority would unapologetically describe themselves as workaholics.

A study of managers in industry found that many of them worked 60-65 hours per week. The willingness to work long, difficult hours has exemplified many powerful leaders. This diligence allows them to pass their competitors … even to overcome others who might be more intelligent or have more skill. In addition, a person's energy will be an example and inspiration for others.

Some successful people have had a "once in a lifetime" break at some point. But, when the chance came, they were already working and were ready to say "yes" to the chance.

In a Ted-Ed Original lesson, Richard St. John coined the word "WorkaFrolic" to define some of these successful people. They enjoy what they are doing so much that WorkaFrolic is a better description than workaholic! They can commit to doing all the hard work because it is something they enjoy doing.

I am not suggesting that working 60-80 hours a week is a great character trait. There may be times when it is necessary – such as if you are starting a new business of your own. But, it is also important to maintain quality in your life, health, and relationships with family, etc. The point is that being diligent and energetic – being a hard worker – is important.

Quotes about Energetic or Diligent

"Diligence is the mother of good fortune." – Miguel de Cervantes Saavedra

"He who labors diligently need never despair; for all things are accomplished by diligence and labor." – Menander

"The dictionary is the only place that success comes before work. Work is the key to success, and hard work can help you accomplish anything." – Vince Lombardi

"Energy and persistence conquer all things." – Benjamin Franklin

"Hard work spotlights the character of people: some turn up their sleeves, some turn up their noses, and some don't turn up at all." – Sam Ewing

"All hard work brings a profit, but mere talk leads only to poverty." – Proverbs 14:23 (New International Version Bible)

"Let us not become weary in doing good, for at the proper time we will reap a harvest if we do not give up." – Galatians 6:9 (New International Version Bible)

Examples of a Person Who Exhibits Energy or Diligence – Modern

Anthony Trollope is considered one of the most prolific and successful novelists of the Victorian era. Every morning, before going to work at the post office, he would get up and write. His goal was 250 words every fifteen minutes for three hours. He continued this for thirty-three years as he wrote more than two dozen novels.

Alexander Graham Bell was an eminent scientist, inventor, and engineer in the late 1800's through his death in 1922. In addition to inventing the telephone, Bell had many other inventions in aeronautics, optical telecommunications, and hydrofoils. As a young man, Bell would often work around the clock and only allow himself three to four hours sleep per night. At times when he was working on a new idea, he would work up to twenty-two hours straight without sleep.

Examples of a Person Who Exhibits Energy or Diligence – Bible

Joseph is an example of a person who exhibited energy and diligence in the Bible. When he was young, Joseph appeared to be a little conceited and caused problems with his brothers. He ended up being sold into slavery. After this, Joseph seemed to turn his life around.

Joseph was sold to Potiphar, an official for Pharaoh. Joseph was such a hard worker that he was promoted to the position of overseer of Potiphar's entire household. *"Potiphar put him in charge of his household, and he entrusted to his care everything he owned."* (Genesis 39:4, New International Version Bible)

After a false accusation, Joseph was thrown into prison. Again, he worked so diligently that he was put in charge of all the prisoners. *"So the warden put Joseph in charge of all those held in the prison, and he was made responsible for all that was done there."* (Genesis 39:22, New International Version Bible)

Joseph ended up staying in prison for a few years, but he was released after interpreting a dream for the Pharaoh. The Pharaoh recognized the wisdom and diligence of Joseph and put him in charge of all of Egypt with only the Pharaoh being above Joseph. *"You shall be in charge of my palace, and all my people are to submit to your orders. Only with respect to the throne will I be greater than you."* (Genesis 41:40, New International Version Bible)

For seven years of plenty Joseph collected the abundance of food and stored it up safely. For the next seven years of famine, Joseph was able to distribute the food to the people in need. *"And all the world came to Egypt to buy grain from Joseph, because the famine was severe everywhere."* (Genesis 41:57, New International Version Bible)

Through these stories, we see that Joseph was an energetic, diligent hard worker, and a skilled administrator.

> **"To be idle is a short road to death and to be diligent is a way of life; foolish people are idle, wise people are diligent." – Buddha**

Cultivating Energy/Diligence

How do you cultivate energy and diligence? Unfortunately, the basic answer is that diligence is like a muscle, and you have to exercise it in order to make it stronger. So, the way to cultivate diligence is to be diligent. Like any muscle, it will grow through practice and repetition. You just have to do it.

Here are a few tips that will help:

- Know your end goal – if you have an end result in mind, you can more easily commit to working hard. The goal gives you a direction. If you have no goals in mind, then you have no reason to commit to work.

- Set smaller goals along the way – as you accomplish the smaller goals, you will gain motivation to continue on to the next goal.

- Track your progress – keep a record as you reach milestones along the way. Again, this will help you gain motivation to keep on keeping on.

- Find something you love, something you are enthusiastic about – if you are enthusiastic about your work, you can push yourself to be diligent about the work required. There will always be difficult parts of the job, but find the things about it that you love. Only when you love it will you be able to put in a whole-hearted effort. You need to love the process as you work towards your goal.

- Stay positive (see the chapter on Winning Attitude) – getting rid of negativity will allow you to stick to the work. Keep the positive end goal in mind, and don't allow pessimism and negativity to take over.

- Believe in yourself – everyone has mental and physical strength. You CAN be a hard worker. It is possible to be diligent. Yes, you can!

R – Responsible

Definitions:

- Responsible: able to make moral or rational decision on one's own and therefore answerable for one's behavior; able to be trusted or depended upon; reliable; accountable as for something within one's power

- Responsibility: the state, quality, or fact of being responsible; the obligation to carry forward an assigned task to a successful conclusion

Being Responsible Is Essential for Winners

Taking responsibility for your own actions is am important trait for a champion … having the mindset of a winner.

It is a tough and courageous path to take responsibility and follow through on your convictions. You will face roadblocks and people who tell you that things are not going to work out. Instead of bowing to these things, a responsible person will just keep forging ahead.

The responsible person will do as promised. They can be considered reliable. People prefer to give their business to those people they can count on … people who are responsible and reliable.

The person who is responsible is trusted by their bosses; this can lead to raises and/or promotions.

The person who is responsible doesn't put things off. If they have a job to do, they will do it. Doing things on time shows they are taking control of their life and showing they can manage things well.

People who are responsible don't make excuses or blame others when things go wrong. They admit their mistakes, determine what happened, and use good judgment to do better in the future.

When your life is not going the way you had hoped, you are the person who is responsible for making things better.

If you have a tough decision to make and have been putting it off, it is time to take responsibility and make that decision and follow through with the actions or face the consequences of it.

Responsible people reap the rewards of their actions eventually. If you want to be viewed as a winner, then step up to the plate and start take action.

Quotes about Responsibility

"The best job goes to the person who can get it done without passing the buck or coming back with excuses." – Napoleon Hill

"Responsibility finds a way. Irresponsibility makes excuses." – Gene Bedley

"It is not only for what we do that we are held responsible, but also for what we do not do." – Jean Baptiste Poquelin Moliére

"Each man is questioned by life; and he can only answer to life by answering for his own life; to life he can only respond by being responsible." – Viktor E. Frankl

"Character – the willingness to accept responsibility for one's own life – is the source from which self-respect springs." – Joan Didion

"Hold yourself responsible for a higher standard than anybody expects of you. Never excuse yourself." – Henry Ward Beecher

"Whoever can be trusted with very little can also be trusted with much, and whoever is dishonest with very little will also be dishonest with much." – Luke 16:10 (New International Version Bible)

Example of a Person Who Exhibits Responsibility – Modern

In 1940, Britain stood alone against the all conquering Nazi war machine. The invasion of Britain looked imminent as Hitler's troops had swept all countries before them. There were several leading British politicians who advocated surrender.

Sir Winston Churchill was steadfast in his refusal to consider defeat, surrender, or a compromise peace. This inspired the nation to fight on and achieve total victory whatever the cost. Five years later, British troops took part in the Allied landings in Normandy and later completed the liberation of Europe.

Churchill said, "The price of greatness is responsibility."

Example of a Person Who Exhibits Responsibility – Bible

Joseph of Nazareth, the earthly father of Jesus, was a carpenter – a skilled craftsman. Joseph was engaged to Mary and found out she was pregnant. He could have sent her away or even had her put to death for the apparent unfaithfulness. However, when God let Joseph know that Mary was not unfaithful and that Joseph was to go through with the marriage, Joseph exhibited responsibility.

Joseph did all that he needed to do to protect Jesus and Mary, even taking them to a foreign country for a time to keep them safe. Joseph taught Jesus the trade of carpentry.

There is not a lot of information about Joseph of Nazareth in the Bible. However, what we see is that Joseph was a good example of a responsible person.

Cultivating Responsibility

You must recognize that – for the most part – you are responsible for your own life. You may have friends and family that help share the burden with you, but at the end of the day you in charge.

Take the time now to think about and write down any areas of your life that are not what they should be. Is your weight getting out of control? Do you hate your job? Are you not making enough money?

When you have finished the list of areas of life that need addressing, think of the ways you can address them … ways you can take responsibility.

"I believe that we are solely responsible for our choices, and we have to accept the consequences of every deed, word, and thought throughout our lifetime."
– Elizabeth Kubler-Ross

Here are two examples:

- *Area needing addressing: I have put on 20 pounds*
  How can I take responsibility: I need to stop eating so much fast food. I am in control of what I put in my mouth.

- *Area needing addressing*: My marriage is struggling
  How can I take responsibility: I need to address the issues with my wife, and instead of always pointing the finger, I need to take responsibility for my own actions.

This will not be an easy exercise because you will have to be painfully honest with yourself. You will have to indicate areas of your life you might not be happy with and then admit that it is in your control to do something. Even if you don't fully believe the problems are purely your responsibility, try to address them as if they were. Recognize that you are totally responsible for your own thoughts, feelings, and actions.

In a blogpost on stage2planning.com, Josh Patrick writes, *"Knowing that I can't control the fact that I have cancer is one thing. Knowing that I can control my thoughts and actions is what matters. Taking responsibility for my life allowed me to do cancer and not have cancer do me."*

The above exercise is a great way to train your mind into taking responsibility for the actions in your life, rather than blaming another person or circumstance. Remember, no matter what the problem is in your life, you have the power to deal with it (even if only to deal with your thoughts and attitude toward the problem). Take responsibility!

"IF YOU COULD KICK THE PERSON IN THE PANTS RESPONSIBLE FOR MOST OF YOUR TROUBLE, YOU WOULDN'T SIT FOR A MONTH."
— THEODORE ROOSEVELT

W – Winning Attitude (Positive Attitude)

Definitions:

- Attitude: the way a person views something or tends to behave toward it; a manner disposition, feeling, or position; a complex mental state involving beliefs and feelings and values and dispositions to act in certain ways

- Positive Attitude: a state of mind that continues to seek, find, and execute ways to win, or find a desirable outcome, regardless of the circumstances; opposes negativity, defeatism, and hopelessness

Having a Winning Attitude (Positive Attitude) Is Essential for Winners

A positive attitude is a trait that you can develop over time. No one is born with a good or bad attitude; you have to make the decision about how you will face life. Unfortunately, too many people walk around with a bad or negative attitude, letting the negative thoughts take over.

Your attitude affects every area of your life: the expression on your face, your body language, the things you say, your work habits, the way you dress, and even your health. The Mayo Clinic reports that a positive attitude can reduce your stress levels.

One way to create a winning (positive) attitude is to try to think about pleasant and constructive things as often as possible. You will come across in that same way (pleasant and constructive). This creates a favorable and lasting impression.

Every time you deal with someone, your attitude shows. If you are gloomy and always in a bad mood, people will view you as a moody person and this reputation will follow you around.

On the other hand, you can have a winning attitude. The person with a winning attitude has a positive mindset and a can-do attitude. When an obstacle presents itself, they automatically begin thinking of ways to work around it. They don't allow anything or anyone to defeat them.

In his book *Strengthening Your Grip*, Charles R. Swindoll writes:

"This may shock you, but I believe the single most significant decision I can make on a day-to-day basis is my choice of attitude. It is more important than my past, my education, my bankroll, my successes or failures, fame or pain, what other people think of me or say about me, my circumstances, or my position. Attitude is that 'single string' that keeps me going or cripples my progress. It alone fuels my fire or assaults my hope. When my attitudes are right, there's no barrier too high, no valley too deep, no dream too extreme, no challenge too great for me."

People with positive attitudes seem to suffer less and recover quicker. Their health is better and they are better liked. Some people will look at them and say, "Well, they have all the luck." However, psychologists say that a winning attitude – a positive attitude – can be learned with practice.

You CAN change your life by thinking more positively and by changing your outlook on life in general. Winners always keep a positive mindset!

Having a positive attitude does not mean that you are ignoring all the bad things in life. However, you choose to focus on the positive and not on the negative.

Take action today and make improving your attitude a priority on your to-do list!

Quotes about a Winning Attitude

"Attitude is a little thing that makes a big difference." – Winston Churchill

"Your attitude, not your aptitude, will determine your altitude." – Zig Ziglar

"Develop an attitude of gratitude, and give thanks for everything that happens to you, knowing that every step forward is a step toward achieving something bigger and better than your current situation." – Brian Tracy

"There is a little difference in people, but that little difference makes a big difference. The little difference is attitude. The big difference is whether it is positive or negative." – W. Clement Stone

"Keep your face always toward the sunshine – and shadows will fall behind you." – Walt Whitman

"Finally, brothers and sisters, whatever is true, whatever is noble, whatever is right, whatever is pure, whatever is lovely, whatever is admirable – if anything is excellent or praiseworthy – think about such things." – Philippians 4:8 (New International Version Bible)

"Give thanks in all circumstances; for this is God's will for you in Christ Jesus." – I Thessalonians 5:18 (New International Version Bible)

Example of a Person Who Exhibits a Winning Attitude – Modern

Bruce Lee has demonstrated throughout his life that he has a positive attitude. Even at the young age of 12, when he was beaten up by a street gang, he remained positive. He was inspired to take up martial arts after this encounter. For the next several years, he studied the art of Wing Chun Kung Fu.

At one point in his life, Bruce Lee had a major back injury due to a weightlifting accident. Although it could have stopped his martial arts career, Bruce Lee kept a positive attitude and worked hard to return to full strength.

Bruce Lee is someone who has always demonstrated a positive attitude in his life and he sums it up beautifully here:

"You have a choice. You are Master of your attitude. Choose the positive, the constructive. Optimism is a faith that leads to success."

Example of a Person Who Exhibits a Winning Attitude – Bible

Ruth is an example from the Bible of someone with a winning attitude. She is from the country of Moab. A man from Bethlehem, along with his wife (Naomi) and two sons moved to Moab. Ruth becomes the wife of one of the sons. After 10 years in Moab, the father and both of the sons died. This left Naomi with two daughters-in-law.

Naomi decides to return to Bethlehem. At first, both daughters-in-law are going to go with her. But Naomi lets them know that it is not necessary for them to back with her. The one daughter-in-law chooses to stay in Moab. But, Ruth had a positive attitude and said she would go with her mother-in-law. *"When Naomi realized that Ruth was determined to go with her, she stopped urging her."* (Ruth 1:18, New International Version Bible)

Ruth determined that she would have a better future. She refused to admit defeat, even though bad things had happened.

When you read the rest of the story, Ruth continues with a winning attitude. She ends up with a new husband who also cares for Ruth's mother-in-law.

Cultivating a Winning Attitude

In his book *Savoring: A New Model of Positive Experience*, Fred B. Bryant writes, "Bad things will come and find you, knock down your door, and make you deal with them. The positive stuff ain't like that. You have to open the door, go hunt for it, and find it."

So, the first step to cultivating a winning attitude is to look for the good things, the positive things that happen each day. At the end of each day, write in your journal at least three positive things that happened during the day. It might be little things, such as "a driver slowed down and let me into the lane as I pulled out from the store." Or, it might be much bigger things. It could be a great testimonial from a client or customer.

If you will do this every day, you will begin to recognize that good things really do happen all the time. You will find it easier to notice the good each day which will make it easier to have a winning attitude all the time.

The second step is to create a "gratitude journal." Far too often people in today's society focus on what they don't have or the things they want to have. Taking a second to appreciate everything you DO have is key to fostering a positive attitude.

> *"I am convinced that life is 10% what happens to me and 90% how I react to it."*
> **– Charles Swindoll**

Don't waste another second taking things for granted. You can start tracking things you are grateful for in the pages of a journal that you will specifically use for this – a gratitude journal. The key here is to not fill in 5 spots and quit. Keep adding to this list indefinitely.

There is one more technique that I found very helpful for my own positive attitude. Consider writing a letter to someone you owe a debt of gratitude (teacher, grandparent, mentor, etc) thanking them for helping you along your way. Studies have shown that this technique measurably boosts people's happiness for more than a month. Follow these steps to help with this exercise:

1. Choose a person

2. What does this person mean to you?

3. How did they help you?

4. What did it teach you?

Once you answer those four questions, you will have the main talking points for your letter.

This letter will not only boost your positive attitude, it will mean the world to whoever receives your letter.

These three exercises can help you boost your positive attitude. I have found these to be the most helpful in a quest for the mindset of a winner. Just remember that YOU can control your attitude.

> *"Our attitudes control our lives. Attitudes are a secret power working twenty-four hours a day, for good or bad. It is of paramount importance that we know how to harness and control this great force."*
> – Irving Berlin

I – Integrity

Definitions:

- Integrity: adherence to moral principles; honesty; soundness of moral character; an undivided or unbroken completeness or totality with nothing wanting

Having Integrity Is Essential for Winners

Notice that one definition of integrity is completeness. A person who has integrity is someone whose core values are the basis for what they say <u>and</u> do <u>and</u> believe. Everything is completely in alignment.

The character trait of integrity is usually seen as synonymous with virtue, moral excellence, ethical decisions, and honorable actions. Integrity is doing the right thing – all the time, no matter who is watching or even if no one is watching, no matter the cost, no matter the hardships, no matter if it will be easy or hard . . . no matter what.

People who show integrity are people that are willing to stand behind their work and their word. When you display integrity those around you will view you as someone they can trust. You will become a role model for others to follow.

Integrity helps you personally, as well as at work. If you possess integrity you don't have to worry about getting caught in lies. You can go about your life with an air of confidence.

A person with integrity naturally shows other traits, which include being self confident; having a strong sense of what they want out of life; assertiveness; trustworthiness; and humility. They seem to be more down-to-earth people.

Quotes about Integrity

"Live so that when your children think of fairness, caring, and integrity, they think of you." – H. Jackson Brown, Jr.

"It's not hard to make decisions when you know what your values are." – Roy Disney, Walt Disney Executive

"Real integrity is doing the right thing, knowing that nobody's going to know whether you did it or not." – Oprah Winfrey

"If you don't have integrity, you have nothing. You can't buy it. You can have all the money in the world, but if you are not a moral and ethical person, you really have nothing." – Henry Kravis

"For we are taking pains to do what is right, not only in the eyes of the Lord but also in the eyes of man." – II Corinthians 8:21 (New International Version Bible)

"Whoever walks in integrity walks securely, but whoever takes crooked paths will be found out." – Proverbs 10:9 (New International Version Bible)

Example of a Person Who Exhibits Integrity – Modern

Abraham Lincoln is a great example of someone who exhibited integrity. He was first called "Honest Abe" as a young man clerking in a store. When he realized he had mistakenly shortchanged a customer by a few pennies, he would close the shop and deliver the correct change, no matter how far he had to walk.

As others recognized his integrity, Abraham Lincoln was called on to act as a judge or mediator in various situations. His judgment was considered final because people relied on his integrity.

When Lincoln began his law practice, he knew that people had a common distrust of lawyers. But, Lincoln counseled potential lawyers to "resolve to be honest at all events."

Gordon Leidner on www.greatamericanhistory.net wrote:

"The Reverend Albert Hale of Springfield's First Presbyterian Church said, 'Abraham Lincoln has been here all the time, consulting and consulted by all classes, all parties, and on all subjects of political interest, with men of every degree of corruption, and yet I have never heard even an enemy accuse him of intentional dishonesty or corruption.'"

When Stephen A Douglas learned that Lincoln was to be his opponent in the race for the presidency, he said, "You have nominated a very able and a very honest man."

There are many other examples from the life of Abraham Lincoln showing that he exhibited integrity throughout his life.

Example of a Person Who Exhibits Integrity – Bible

Nebuchadnezzar, king of Babylon, captured several young Israelite men. One of these young men was Daniel. The captured young men are to be put to work in the king's palace. They are to have training for three years and then put into the king's service.

Daniel does not want to "defile" himself with the king's food and drink. He has integrity and does not want to go against his beliefs. Daniel offers an alternative to the overseer which will allow Daniel to keep his integrity. The overseer agrees, and Daniel is able to continue to live by his beliefs.

There are several other examples through Daniel's life where he is able to maintain his integrity in the face of opposition.

Cultivating Integrity

We discussed above that integrity is completeness. This is the ability to be consistent in your actions, values and principles. If consistency to your values and principles is a cornerstone of integrity then you better know what yours are!

Before you go any further, take the time to think of three - five values or principles that you feel strongly about (examples: treating all people fairly, honor, compassion). Think of things that you believe in so much that you won't waver from them.

Now that you have these values written down, it is time to show your integrity by sticking to them in the face of opposition. Make a commitment to yourself to always live and work according to your values.

You also need to make sure that your personal and career goals are in line with the values. If not, then you need to evaluate your life. If there are areas of your life that are not in line with your values, find the reason and decide what needs to change.

Remember, integrity is always being whole – what you say, what you do, and what you believe – everything in line with your values, all the time. Always walk your talk.

> *"The supreme quality for leadership is unquestionably integrity. Without it, no real success is possible, no matter whether it is on a section gang, a football field, in an army, or in an office."*
> – Dwight D. Eisenhower

N – Never Give Up/Persistent

Definitions:

- Persistent: refusing to give up or let go; unrelenting

- Persistence: the quality of being persistent; tenacity

Never Giving Up and Being Persistent Is Essential for Winners

The idea of persistence in this chapter is continuing to do something or try to do something even though it is difficult ... continuing beyond the usual or the expected.

Persistence is important in your life because it allows you to identify those things you want and then focus on achieving them no matter what. An example would be a person who has a sore leg, but pushes through the last mile of their walk.

Never giving up – being persistent – is going to help you be a success in your life. When things go wrong, you will focus back on your target, find a way around or through the obstacle, and continue on toward the goal.

Facing the challenge is part of persistence. The core of being persistent is continuing toward the goal in spite of problems or obstacles.

Persistence is difficult in the world of instant gratification. We have fast food, instant messaging, speed dating, etc. Statistics.com says the average attention span in 2013 was 8 seconds! (The average attention span of a goldfish is 9 seconds.) People want their goal to be accomplished in the time it takes to go through the drive-through at the local McDonalds. It is important to recognize that there are things worth waiting for! Never Giving Up/Persistence – even when the success is far off – is the key.

People who are persistent learn how to confront challenges, learn to assess these challenges, and then find workable solutions to them. Regardless of the amount of time this takes, persistent people will work tirelessly until they have reached their goal. These are seen as admirable leadership qualities.

Everyone can strive to reach their goals, and it is the persistent people who rise to the top undefeated. You must decide if you are going to be one of these people or if the path to your success is too much of a struggle?

Quotes about Never Giving Up or Persistence

"Most of the important things in the world have been accomplished by people who have kept on trying when there seemed to be no hope at all." – Dale Carnegie

"Patience, persistence, and perspiration make an unbeatable combination for success." – Napoleon Hill

"Ambition is the path to success, persistence is the vehicle you arrive in." – William Eardley IV

"If you do not have persistence then no amount of education, talent or genius can make up for it." – Stephen Richards

"Big shots are only little shots who keep shooting." – Christopher Morley

"Let us not become weary in doing good, for at the proper time we will reap a harvest if we do not give up." – Galatians 6:9 (New International Version Bible)

Example of a Person Who Exhibits Never Giving Up or Persistence – Modern

Nelson Mandela was the son of a tribal King in the Madiba clan in Transkei, South Africa. Mandela chose to become a lawyer so he could make a contribution to the struggles of his people.

He was expelled from college for joining in a student protest. Instead of quitting, he went to a different college and completed his BA. Mandela had to battle against the South African apartheid system which didn't make things any easier for him. He finally was able to practice law and helped establish South Africa's first black law firm.

Although Mandela spent many years in prison, he helped many black South Africans survive in the apartheid system.

Even though the apartheid system was powerful in South Africa, Nelson Mandela played a vital role in ending it. He was responsible for bringing about the first real democratic elections and was inaugurated as South Africa's first democratically elected President.

Without his persistence, the change in his country might never have happened.

Example of a Person Who Exhibits Never Giving Up or Persistence – Bible

Jesus traveled throughout the land teaching and healing. Some men had a friend who was paralyzed. When Jesus came to their town, the men wanted to take their friend to Jesus so the man could be healed. Unfortunately, the people had gathered in such huge numbers that the house (where Jesus was teaching) was totally packed. Mark 2:2

says that people gathered in such great numbers, "that there was no room left, not even outside the door."

The friends would not give up. *"Since they could not get him to Jesus because of the crowd, they made an opening in the roof above Jesus by digging through it and then lowered the mat the man was lying on."* (Mark 2:4, New International Version Bible)

That is persistence!

Jesus rewarded their persistence and their faith by healing their friend.

Cultivating Persistence

Building persistence is not something that is going to happen overnight. However, the good news is that persistence is like a muscle: the more you use it, the more it grows.

The first step towards persistence is similar to the first step towards ambition. You must define some of your goals. If you don't even know what you are working towards, how can you work toward it passionately?

For ambition, you were asked to envision the big picture – what life will be like when you have success. For persistence, you will break it down to more specific goals.

Right now, before moving on, write down 3 specific life goals that you want to work towards – be as specific as possible. You can focus on any area of your life. Often people set goals that relate to things like finances, business, health, family and leisure.

An example of a specific goal would be, "I will lose 50 pounds by March 1.

Once you have defined three goals, you have something to focus your persistence on! Now, you have to practice persistence … stubbornly work toward these goals.

One thing that will be helpful is to break the goals down to smaller steps which can be reached more quickly. Instead of 50 pounds by March 1, focus on 3 pounds by the end of the month. Having some success will help you stick to your plans.

To help you further, look at the goals you have written down and list potential "persistence pitfalls". Be proactive and try to identify things that will potentially sabotage your goals. For example, if your goal is weight loss, a potential pitfall might be an upcoming birthday party and all the tempting food.

In addition, write down any solutions you can think of. For the upcoming birthday party, a possible solution would be to budget your calories the week before, so you have some more room to enjoy yourself!

You won't be able to predict every problem, but you can predict some of the obvious ones. This will help you prepare to be persistent! If you know the obstacles that you might face, you can develop strategies to overcome them. Overcoming obstacles is basically persistence in a nutshell!

At the end of the day, the only way to build persistence is to use it!

> *"Nothing in the world can take the place of persistence. Talent will not; nothing is more common than unrewarded talent. Education alone will not; the world is full of educated failures. Persistence alone is omnipotent."*
> — Calvin Coolidge

S – Spirituality

Definitions:

- Spiritual: relating to the spirit or soul and not to physical nature or matter

- Spirituality: concerned with things of the spirit; state, quality, manner or fact of being spiritual

Having Spirituality Is Essential for Winners

When you Google "character traits of winners," spirituality is not included on as many of the lists as the other traits in this book. However, life is more than just mind and body; there is also spirit or soul. So, it is important to recognize this and seek to understand why spirituality is important for everyone.

Dr. Richard Harmer, PhD has done scientific research on the subject of spirituality. His research (reported on http://noetic.org) finds that spirituality makes human life more vibrant, provides a sense of morality and ethics, and allows people to find peace in the midst of life's trials and tribulations. Christopher G. Ellison and Daisy Fan, in their study "Daily Spiritual Experiences and Psychological Well-Being Among US Adults" found that spirituality causes a wide array of positive health outcomes, including "morale, happiness, and life satisfaction."

Engaging Spirituality by JustFaith Ministries asks:

"What moves you deeply, guides your thoughts and actions? What lies at the heart and center of your world?

"Spirituality fuels our life-long journey to God, source and wellspring of life.

"We could also describe it as the deep motivating force for our lives. In this sense, spirituality determines the quality of our being. Whether we are aware of it or not, we all operate out of some kind of spirituality. Jesus explained it as 'where you put your heart.'"

Spirituality and faith are often spoken of together. Everyone has faith. Some people have faith in themselves, in their own abilities, their money, or their job. Some people have faith in the government. Some people have faith in their families or loved ones. All of these things are temporary and can disappoint. Relationships end, health fails, jobs are lost, and governments are overthrown. However, when faith is in God, He can be depended on. God will never leave or forsake those who belong to Him (Deuteronomy 31:6 and Hebrews 13:5; New International Version Bible).

Spirituality may involve organized religion, but in this book, the definition is much more personal. Spirituality recognizes that God is actively involved in the world and intimately involved with us at all times and in all places. God is personal and present for us.

The person who exhibits spirituality is seeking to know God, to love and respect God, and to find the deeper significance in life through their relationship with God. As a person comes to know God personally through Jesus, they will have God's Spirit living within them. This means an even more intimate relationship with God.

> **"We are not human beings having a spiritual experience. We are spiritual beings having a human experience."**
> **– Pierre Teilhard de Chardin**

Dr. Glen Scorgie on www.biblicaltraining.org says that Christian Spirituality is:

- encountering the living God and being renewed in Christ-likeness,

- holistic: living all of life before God, and

- life lived in the presence and power of the Holy Spirit

True spirituality is not a strictly inward or introspective activity. As we grow closer to God and become more like Christ, we realize that we must be like Him in reaching out to our neighbor. Christian spirituality involves a connectedness to others in addition to connecting to God. With true Christian Spirituality, we will be renewing inwardly, worshipping upwardly, and serving outwardly.

Quotes about Spirituality

"God is closer to me then I am to myself." – Augustine

"I don't understand Christianity. I don't understand electricity either, but I don't intend to sit in the dark until I do." – Unknown

"Science is not only compatible with spirituality; it is a profound source of spirituality." – Carl Sagan

"What you are is God's gift to you, what you become is your gift to God." – Hans Urs von Balthasar

"The spiritual life does not remove us from the world but leads us deeper into it" – Henri J.M. Nouwen

"You can be unbelievably fit in a physical sense, but if you are not connected spiritually you lack a wholeness that undermines your actuality and potential as a complete person." – Rich Roll

"But seek first his kingdom and his righteousness, and all these things will be given to you as well." – Matthew 6:44 (New International Version Bible)

Example of a Person Who Exhibits Spirituality – Modern

Joni Eareckson Tada was born in 1949 in Baltimore, Maryland. She grew up enjoying all kinds of physical activities: riding horses, hiking, playing tennis, and swimming. In July 1967, she misjudged the shallowness of the water as she dove into Chesapeake Bay and broke her neck becoming a quadriplegic, paralyzed from the shoulders down.

According to her best-selling autobiography, *Joni*, she struggled through two years of rehabilitation experiencing anger, depression, suicidal thoughts, and religious doubts. Despite all the difficulties, Tada has become an exceptional witness to the truth that God is available and giving comfort through the most difficult of times.

Tada founded Joni and Friends, and organization providing Christian ministry in the disabled community throughout the world. She served on the National Council on Disability under two Presidents, and has served on many boards and committees for religious organizations. Tada has written over fifty books, sold her artwork painted with a brush held between her teeth, recorded numerous musical albums, and starred in an autobiographical movie of her life.

The Joni and Friends organization has expanded beyond what Tada ever expected, serving more people and providing more services than she ever dreamed. Even with all the growth and changes, Tada says, "it has never deviated from its original purpose of sharing the hope of God's love with a segment of the world's population that is often overlooked and ostracized."

Tada and her husband Ken recently published a book after thirty years of marriage titled *Joni & Ken: An Untold Love Story*. Through sharing the story of their marriage and all the issues it has involved, they hope to speak to the hearts of couples who struggle in their own marriages. She shares, "God has used every trial, every hurt and heartache to entwine us far more intimately than we ever dreamed on the day we married."

Through the years, Tada's life continues to offer inspiration to millions of people around the world that a living and meaningful relationship with God – true spirituality – is more lasting and significant than anything else in life.

Example of a Person Who Exhibits Spirituality – Bible

Paul is a prominent name in the New Testament. He traveled extensively throughout the lands of the Bible teaching the message of God's salvation. He is the author of almost half of the books in the New Testament.

Paul faced many hardships, including shipwrecks, imprisonments, beatings, etc. Yet through it all, Paul's testimony was, *"I can do all this through him who gives me strength."* (Philippians 4:13)

Paul's desire was to know God. In Philippians 3:8, Paul said, *"What is more, I consider everything a loss because of the surpassing worth of knowing Christ Jesus my Lord."* And, two verses later, in Philippians 3:10, Paul wrote, *"I want to know Christ – yes, to know the power of His resurrection."*

In addition to wanting to know God for himself, Paul also wanted to share the knowledge with others. In Colossians 2:2, Paul wrote, *"My goal is that they may be encouraged in heart and united in love, so that they may have the full riches of complete understanding, in order that they may know the mystery of God, namely, Christ."*

Cultivating Spirituality

As we said above, Spirituality involves growing closer to God. This does not always mean that you need to go into a separate place, alone and quiet, in order to find God. God is active everywhere and personal with us. If we will truly look, we can find evidence of God all around us: in the beauty of nature, in relationships with family and friends, in our work, and even in the mundane tasks of daily living. As Brother Lawrence, a 17th century lay brother in a French Monastery wrote in *The Practice of the Presence of God*, we can recognize and practice the presence of God even while washing dishes.

So, step one in cultivating spirituality is to live with awareness. Be willing and open to seeing God's presence in your daily life.

Step two involves making a commitment and maintaining a focus on spirituality. This will involve daily rituals and study. It may be for very short periods when you begin. But take time each day to read from God's Word (the Bible), to listen for His Spirit to guide you, to talk to Him about what is happening in your life.

There will always be distractions to pull you away from pursuing spirituality. You have to make the decision – the commitment – to stick with it.

(There is more information in the Appendix concerning the good news of God in Christ and what it means for you.)

> **"Set your minds on things above, not on earthly things."**
> – Colossians 3:2
> (New International Version Bible)

Conclusion

By now you have discovered some of the top character traits that are consistently shown among people who are seen as winners! Unlike your fingerprints which never change, you can create your character. You can create the mindset of a winner for yourself.

This can be displayed in a variety of ways including running a responsible business, helping out a charitable cause, and having the dedication and determination to follow through on your actions and convictions.

Always be willing to share the knowledge that you have with others. When you can display all of these traits truthfully each and every day, then you will have become a person with the mindset of a winner.

As I said in the introduction, thank you for reading this book. I hope you have gained many insights that will help you be seen as a winner and be prepared for excellence!

Feel free to connect with me on my website at:

http://www.PrepareForExcellence.com

Sherry M. Carroll

Resources

http://addicted2success.com - Addicted2Success's mission is to empower and inspire people by spreading knowledge of self development and life changing stories to the world. They also provide motivational videos, interviews, audio and more.

http://www.success.com - Success Magazine is an inspirational and instructional website offering guidance and insight into improving one's entire life. The website focuses on five key areas for achieving success: business, relationships, wealth, well-being and making a difference.

http://successmindset.us - is an online publication helping aspiring achievers around the world to be successful in their personal and professional life. They're sharing success tips, ideas, stories and resources from some of the success experts around the world.

http://truthfamilylikes.com/successstore - A store with books, cds, dvds, magazines, etc. related to success in business, relationships, wealth, well-being, and making a difference.

Appendix

I am a Christian. I believe the Bible, I pray, I fellowship with other believers, and I am active in my local church. I know that not all of the readers of this book believe the same, and that is your choice. However, my desire is that all of you will have Christ live in your hearts by faith, and that you will come to know and understand how wide and long and high and deep is the love of Christ, and that you will know this love that surpasses all knowledge, so that you may be filled with the fullness of God (from Ephesians 3:18-19, New International Version Bible).

The gospel – the good news – is available to everyone. Here is an excerpt from *Simplify Your Spiritual Life* by Donald S. Whitney which explains a little more about Christian Spirituality and the gospel:

"Christian spirituality begins with one of the most important words in the Bible. That word is gospel, which is the English translation of the New Testament Greek word that literally means "good news." ...

"One of the places where the Bible summarizes the gospel is in 1 Corinthians 15:1-8. The heart of this passage tells us 'Christ died for our sins according to the Scriptures, and that He was buried, and that He rose again on the third day according to the Scriptures' (verses 3-4). So the gospel that produces genuine Christian spirituality is that Jesus Christ died, taking the guilt of sinners and the wrath of God upon Himself, and was raised bodily from the dead to show that the Father accepted His death for others and removed their sins. Christ's substitutionary death for sinners is the measure of His love and His resurrection from the dead is the stunning confirmation that all He said and did is true.

"This is good news—the best possible news—because it demonstrates, among so many other things, the willingness of the God we had sinned against countless times to draw us to Himself, to engage in an intimate relationship with us. It means that He has done in Christ what we couldn't have done for ourselves, opening

the door for us to come in faith and to experience all the indescribable riches of fellowship with God, and thereby become "partakers of the divine nature" (2 Peter 1:4).

"Do you know – by experience – this good news?"

The book *Simplify Your Spiritual Life: Spiritual Disciplines for the Overwhelmed* is available on Amazon.com. Here is a shortcut link to the book on Amazon: http://www.truthfamilylikes.com/simplify.

> "*God is not a belief to which you give your assent. God becomes a reality whom you know intimately, meet everyday, one whose strength becomes your strength, whose love, your love. Live this life of the presence of God long enough and when someone asks you, 'Do you believe there is a God?' you may find yourself answering, 'No, I do not believe there is a God. I know there is a God.'*" – Ernest Boyer, Jr.

www.ingramcontent.com/pod-product-compliance
Lightning Source LLC
Chambersburg PA
CBHW071830020426
42331CB00007B/1675